MW00982238

INTRODUCTION
WORDS OF LOVE

I am delighted to have the privilege of writing the introduction to "Words of Love" by Terrence. I eagerly awaited the publishing of this poetry book.

Some may be skeptical that poets could still be writing love poems. After all, for centuries romantics have been expressing their thoughts in verse and rhyme and surely we should have run out of couplets and soliloquies by now. However, the Greeks have five words for love that when coupled with the endless combinations and types of lovers, provides the poet with endless possibilities.

Their first word is Eros, the root of the word erotic. These are the words of the young lovers, the new lovers. Their poems are full of lust and passion, hot and spicy. These poems hold nothing back and leave little to the imagination. They sing and shout of the adventure of love.

Next is Mania, maybe obsession is a better word. This love is described as possessive and obsessive and these poems will cry out with apologies and promises and pleadings to give their love one more try, as the writer could no longer sleep, think or go on without their lover.

The third word Philos, is the friendship love. A bond shared between brothers or sisters or long lost friends can evoke poetry about family values, memories of growing up. The back yard or the school yard is the beginnings of the stories that these love poems share.

Storgy is the fourth word and describes a motherly love. We can all think of amazing poetry we composed for our mothers on Valentine's Day construction paper or inside the handmade Mother's Day cards. Of course the words from our mothers are always poetry and not soon forgotten.

The last word is Agape. This love is a love that we don't expect to be returned. The poetry we see here is the caregiver feeding the Alzheimer patient; the husband of fifty years making the daily trip to the rest home, or the volunteers working tirelessly in the food banks or the homeless shelters. Or most important, the love we have for our enemies that sets us free though we see no return. These poems are poems of forgiveness and hope and tell of a never ending love.

They are all displayed here in one form or another, each one making its own fragile attempt at explaining that elusive feeling, love.

To all you young lovers, whatever your age, find a cozy, quiet spot, sit back, relax and join us on that endless quest for the perfect love.

Jim McGregor
Feature Writer for the Langley Times Newspaper

INDEX

A HEART OF PAIN 1

A DANCING WARMTH ACROSS MY SOUL 2

A FLOWER AND A SONG 3

A HEART DOTH CRY 4

A HEART JUST LIKE GOD 5

A LETTER TO A FRIEND 6

ALL OVER AGAIN 8

A SIMPLE THING 9

A SONG OF LOVE 11

A SWEET EMBRACE 12

A THOUGHTFUL BLUSH 13

A WEDDING VOW 14

ADORING YOU 16

AN ANGEL IS MY BELOVED 18

AN ODE TO LOVE 19

BECAUSE 21

CINDERELLA WAITRESS 22

DAWN 25

DESTINY 26

FATE AND THE HEART 28

FILLING UP WITH LOVE 29

FLOWERS GENTLE BENEATH OUR FEET* 30

FOR THE LOVE OF YOU 32

FROM WHENCE DID THIS LOVE SPRING 33

HAPPINESS 35

HOW CAN I SAY I LOVE YOU 36

HOW MUCH LOVE CAN ONE HEART HOLD? 37

I LOVE YOU 38

I MISS MY LITTLE SISTER* 39

I'M SMITTIN' 41

IN THE SHADOW OF THE SETTING SUN* 42

INFINITE TRUST 43

JUST A FEW FLOWERS...44

LOVE BEFORE A SONG...46

MY BELOVED...47

MY BELOVED, MY PIANO AND ME 48

MY LAST TRUE LOVE...50

OBSESSION 52

ONCE UPON A TIME 53

ONE SOLITARY LIFE 56

ONE SUNLIT MORN 58

PERFECT LOVE* 59

PINK SHOES 60

POETRY AND LOVE 61

SEEING YOU WITHOUT ME 62

SLEEP WALKING 64

SWEET LAUGHTER 65

THE DAY YOU WENT AWAY..66

THE HARBOUR OF MY HEART 67

THE ALCOHOLIC AND THE HUG.....................................68

THE KISS 70

THE MORNING DAWN..71

THE NIGHT THE BIRDS SANG...72

THE VOICE OF AN ANGEL 73

THE WAVE UPON THE SHORE 74

THEY DON'T KNOW HOW 76

TRUE LOVE..77

TWILIGHT..78

WAKE ME NOT 79

WALKING THE HIGHWAYS AND THE BYWAYS 80

WHAT I SAW..81

WHERE HAVE YOU GONE? 82

WHISPERING EYES..83

WHO ELSE 85

YOUR EYES 86

YOUR HAND IN MINE 87

*** Poems by Jim McGregor can be found
on pages 22, 52, and 64***

THE OBEDIENCE FACTOR

ABOUT THE AUTHOR 91

DEDICATION 93

THE "WOW" FACTOR..94

THE OBEDIENCE FACTOR...96

A HEART OF PAIN

OH WHAT PAIN SUFFERS MY HEART
WHEN UPON THE EVENING WE ARE APART
ALTHOUGH MY HEART DOTH SEARCH IN VAIN
NOT A WORD OR SIGH DOTH EASE MY PAIN

WHEN ONCE I AWOKE UPON THE MORN
WITH ABANDONED HEART SAD AND FORLORN
WITH TEARFUL EYE AND BROKEN HEART
I LAMENT THE DAY THAT WE DID PART

ONE DAY YET OUR GOD WILL SPEAK
AND I WILL FEEL YOUR BREATH UPON MY CHEEK
AS TWILIGHT PEEKS BENEATH A SKY SO GRAND
WE WILL EMBRACE AS ONE AS GOD DID PLAN

Terrence Morrissey
March 2 2010

A DANCING WARMTH ACROSS MY SOUL

Why doth my heart suffer with an ache so intense?
That I scarce can breathe,
Whenever you enter upon my mind
Your beauty enchants my very being
And casts a spell 'round about me
The delicate cast of your beauty
Has captured me forever
Your shadow, like the setting sun
Casts a dancing warmth across my soul

By Terrence Morrissey
Copyright 2009

A FLOWER AND A SONG

Sleepily, one morning, I saw a figure
walking in my garden
She walked amongst a garden bouquet of flowers
Captivating were the flowers arrayed
in a thousand colors
The figure, standing alone, was
so much more beautiful

An enchanting fragrance slowly lifted to the sun
The figure, moving as in a dream,
smiled an entrancing smile
A love song satisfied the morning
quiet from a lone songbird
Alas the song of the shadowy figure was all the sweeter

The shadow, slightly turning, saw
me gazing upon her beauty
Now smiling a smile of loveliness, cast
over a disappearing shoulder
Vanished, as a song bird called, once
again, among the flowers
In an instant my heart joined in a song of happiness

Terrence Morrissey
Copyright 2009

A HEART DOTH CRY

WHY SAY YE, A HEART CANNOT CRY

SURELY IT BLEEDS DOES IT NOT?

WHAT THEN IS THIS FEELING IN MY CHEST

IS IT NOT BUT A TEARDROP
FROM A BROKEN HEART?

By Terrence Morrissey
Copyright 2009

A HEART JUST LIKE GOD

The sun kissed your cheek one early morn
As a gentle breeze caressed your sweet face
A blossom bloomed as you walked by
And a thousand bouquets burst upon the scene

My heart was jealous of all these things
Because they had that moment with you
But wait! I exclaimed one day
As I stood with rejoicing in my heart

God has sent the sun to kiss your cheek
He sent a gentle breeze to caress your sweet face
He made the blossom bloom as you walked by
All because you have a heart just like God

Terrence Morrissey
Copyright 2008

A LETTER TO A FRIEND

Dear Maureen*

I just wanted to drop you a line to let you know how much you have touched me and many others with your story and to thank you for your courage and your refusal to give up in the face of adversity.

A MAGNIFICENT GRAND PIANO IS WHAT ALL THE PEOPLE WANT TO PLAY BUT WHEN THEY TRY TO PLAY THIS BEAUTIFUL PIANO WITHOUT KNOWING ONE KEY FROM ANOTHER ALL THE SONGS AND MUSIC JUST COME OUT WRONG.

I REMEMBER WHEN YOU FIRST ARRIVED A YEAR AGO YOU KIND OF REMINDED ME OF AN OLD UPRIGHT THAT HAD BEEN STORED IN THE BASEMENT FOR YEARS. THERE WASN'T A CHANCE THAT ANY MUSIC AT ALL COULD COME OUT OF IT NOT EVEN ANY PLAIN OLD MUSIC, NOT A CHANCE.

HERE IT IS, ONE YEAR LATER AND THAT OLD PIANO HAS BEEN DUSTED OFF AND THE KEYS ALL MADE SHINY AND UNDERNEATH ALL THE DUST ALL THOSE YEARS WAS HIDDEN THE GRANDEST PIANO OF THEM ALL.

NOW SITTING AT THE KEYBOARD OF YOUR LIFE, MAKING THE SWEETEST SOUND THAT ANY HUMAN HAS EVER HEARD IS YOUR HIGHER

POWER. WHAT GOD HAS DONE WITH THAT OLD DUSTY PIANO IS NOTHING SHORT OF A MIRACLE. BECAUSE OF YOUR WILLINGNESS TO TURN ALL THE SONGS OF YOUR LIFE OVER TO GOD YOU NOW THRILL US WITH A NEW SONG AND HOW SWEET THAT SOUND IS.

THANK YOU FOR BEING YOU AND BLESSING ALL OF US WITH YOUR STORY....YOUR MIRACLE.... AND YOUR HAPPINESS.

WE ARE ALL THE BETTER FOR KNOWING YOU.

Warmest Regards,

Terrence Morrissey

> *On the occasion of an AA member's first year birthday of sobriety. Unfortunately she passed away one year later.

ALL OVER AGAIN

My precious beloved
Today I fell in love with you, all over again
I loved you from the moment our eyes first met
And I loved you more when our lips first touched
How blessed I am to have you in my life
And how blessed I am to call you 'My Beloved'
Thank you for loving me
For tomorrow I will fall in love with you
ALL OVER AGAIN

Terrence Morrissey

A SIMPLE THING

Why shed a teardrop over such a simple thing?
I ask myself as I lay there by your side.
Reaching out I touched you and you turned to face me,
Our lips met and the teardrops on
my cheek mingled with yours.

In an instant I knew from whence came the teardrop,
It came from the depth of my very being.
Holding back nothing I let the teardrops flow,
Shame overtook me, men aren't supposed to cry.

Reaching out once again, I touched
your soft, sweet self,
As before our lips met, one again
your tears mingled with mine.
The gentleness of your kiss told me
that my tears were not in vain,
For you knew and understood why
my pain was so great.

Never have I loved so completely
or with such abandon,
Out of the deep recesses of your heart I heard a song,
There in the darkness your song became my song,
Two hearts beat as one and the
pain in my heart exploded.

When I told you that I loved you completely,
You whispered softly, 'I know you
do,' and I was fulfilled.
Thank you my beloved for giving yourself to me
And letting me give myself to you.

By Terrence Morrissey
Copyright January 2008

A SONG OF LOVE

I FOUND MY HEART SINGING A SONG OF LOVE
A LOVE SONG THAT I NEVER HEARD BEFORE
LINGERING IN MY VERY HEART AND SOUL
IT SPOKE OF YOUR BEAUTY
AND MY LOVE FOR YOU

FROM WHENCE IT CAME I KNOW NOT
FOR I AM YET TO MEET YOU, TO EMBRACE YOU
I KNOW YOU ARE THERE FOR
I FEEL YOUR SPIRIT
AS YOU GLANCE ACROSS A CROWDED ROOM

I WANT TO FEEL YOUR TOUCH,
AS I FEEL YOUR LOVE
BUT I KNOW NOT WHO YOU ARE
DESTINY AWAITS ME AS YOU
SMILE A SILENT SMILE
I TURN AND YOUR SONG REACHES
OUT TO EMBRACE ME

By Terrence Morrissey
Copyright January 2009

A SWEET EMBRACE

Oh what pain doth break upon my heart
When alas I find we both must part
Where goest the joy of a heart unfulfilled
When alas the beauty of your voice is stilled

What strange encounter have I with thee
As the sun doth set beyond the sea
Come my beloved arise and faint not
As in my arms where forever sought

The sunlit tresses of your hair so fine
As gentle as the fragrance of the sweetest wine
For in my breast beats a heart so wild
With thee forever as one beguiled

Hold thee my love within thy breast
For in your holding my heart doth rest
A waning smile across your face
Forever held in a sweet embrace

By Terrence Morrissey
Copyright 2009

A THOUGHTFUL BLUSH

I saw you walking in the pale moonlight

And the rose you planted in the garden of my heart

When once we were lovers,

Blushed a thoughtful blush

And watered by the tears of a broken heart

The rose lives on

By Terrence Morrissey
July 2011

A WEDDING VOW
(My Promise to You)

This is my promise to you, my beloved
That as long as you allow me
I will cherish you and honour you
In all of the things I say and do

My promise is as faithful as the sunrise
As long lasting as the skies above
It shines more brilliant than the brightest star
Never to falter whether I am near or far

For my darling if I promise in the words of man
My pledge is as weak as the weakest child
But my word is shrouded in the
love of an honourable man
You can count on it always to be valiant and true

What good would I be if I could move a mountain?
Or swim the largest ocean, or be the slayer of dragons
Or bear the whole world upon my
shoulders for all to see
And yet fail you and render my promise barren

No, my beloved I will love you with patience
I will boast of God's gift to me, which is you
I will not seek my own fulfilment
but yours first, always
In troubled times I will persevere and
our God will see me through

You have made my life favoured, even
more precious that breath itself
Your kindness and tenderness have
won me utterly, forever
If you wear this ring that comes with
a promise of my undying love
I now do commit to you my life,
completely and forever

When the trials of life and love overtake us
And around us the waters are disquieted
Invading even our very souls
I will fall to my knees and call upon our God

And He will deliver us into calmness and peace
For His promise is the greatest promise of all
That never will our God forsake us or leave us
His love is the strength that I will call upon
To keep my promise to you, my beloved

By Terrence Morrissey
Copyright 2009

ADORING YOU

How do I adore you, you might ask
And I, scarcely breathing, would answer
Let me kiss you with the kisses of my mouth
For your kiss is more delightful
than a morning's sunrise

Your cheeks, aflame with the color of
passion, are as velvet to touch
The fragrance of your perfume sets
my soul and body aflame
How breathtaking are your eyes, careless and seductive
How wonderful you are, a delicate and beautiful flower

When at twilight I hold you in my arms
I drink of your sweetness as at a banquet
I am aroused by your very being,
Our eyes meet and love is held for eternity

Your smile captivates me and beckons me closer
I reach out and in a twinkling we are one
You fade into my very existence, our lips touch
Our bodies, inseparable, are as one

All night long upon our bed, we speak
of beautiful days to come
Of future torrid nights and dreams yet to redeem
Once more you rise up to meet me
and our bodies are as one
Gently you sigh that you love me and
I whisper that I adore you
And in an instant we are paradise bound

By Terrence Morrissey
Copyright 2009

*Adapted from 'Song of Solomon' King
James Version of the Bible.

AN ANGEL IS MY BELOVED

You are like an angel in the garden of my dreams
You are as lovely as a sunset across a lake of blue
You are as pretty as the first flower of spring
You are as gentle as an angel sent from God

Your smile has captivated me since first we met
Your love circles my heart as a rainbow circles heaven
Your touch is as calming as the kiss of a child
Your eyes sparkle as a dew drop on a misty morn

I hold the memory of our first embrace
Buried deep within this heart of mine
The memory of your lips touching mine
Is as fresh as the memory of the first snow of winter

As I contemplate the last flicker of a candle
And the last rays of sun on a summer evening
Or the rising of the moon across a calming lake
I see an angel, and that angel is my beloved

Terrence Morrissey
Copyright 2009

AN ODE TO LOVE

I was thinking, as I sat beside a stream
Of all the ways I could say that I love you
But alas no thought came to mind

I stood and walked beside a field of flowers
And thought of all the ways I could say that I love you
But alas no thought came to mind

Resting beneath a tree so grand
I contemplated all the ways I could say I love you
But alas no thought came to mind

I looked upon the sky so grand
And pursued the words that would say I love you
But alas, no words came to mind

Closing my eyes I saw your face before me
And I knew of the words to say I love you
And the words came finally to my mind

The gentleness of your smile, the
kindness in your heart
The beauty in your eyes, the loveliness of your face
Spoke across the heavens all the
reasons why I love my beloved

The stream did flow, the flowers did bloom
The tree stood majestic and tall unbending
The clouds billowed in a flawless sky

All of these things spoke the words I could not find
To tell you how much I love you
It was God who spoke in his creation
how much I love you

Terrence Morrissey
February 6, 2011

BECAUSE

YOU ARE SO BEAUTIFUL
THAT WHEN YOU SMILED

I WAS IN ONE BREATHTAKING MOMENT,
TRANSPORTED TO A HEAVENLY PLACE

WHEN GOD CREATED THE LAUGHTER IN YOU
HE CREATED IT AFTER THE SOUND
OF AN ANGEL'S SONG

WHEN YOUR SMILE, BEAUTY AND
LAUGHTER COME TOGETHER
AT THAT VERY MOMENT ALL EARTH'S
CREATURES ARE STILLED

AND THE WHOLE OF HEAVEN REJOICES

BECAUSE

YOU ARE SO VERY BEAUTIFUL

Terrence Morrissey
Copyright 2009

CINDERELLA WAITRESS

I pulled into a little town
Arriving too late to unload:
I parked my truck in an empty lot
By a dusty gravel road;
I found a late night restaurant
With a young girl working there,
She smiled at me a tired smile
And pulled a pencil from her hair;
She said 'Mister don't you take to0 long
To put your order in,
Cause it's only half an hour
Til the dancing will begin.'

'And you might think I'm crazy
After being on my feet all day,
The only place I find my sanity
Is that Country Cabaret!'

So I downed my hash and coffee
And I followed her to town;
Ketchup stains had turned to sequins
On a Cinderella county gown;
As she walked through those swinging doors,
The crowd let out a cheer;
The man up on the bandstand cried,
"The line dance teacher's here!"
She yelled "Loosen up your collars folks,
The evening might get hot;
Bring your partners to the dance floor
'Cause there's a lesson to be taught!"

And I thought that gal was crazy
After being on her feet all day;
Her glass slippers turned to cowboy boots
So she could dance the night away!

Now a hundred people took the floor
And started slidin side by side;
Another hundred stood and cheered
A hundred more lined up outside;
They never took their eyes off her
Just glued to every move;
Stompin, slidin, spinning, glidin
Like she was in a groove;
She shouted out instructions
As she circled through the crowd,
And when the song was over,
She curtsied and she bowed!

They didn't know that girl was crazy,
That she'd been on her feet all day,
So she taught them every dance step
That country band could play!

She put her hands up on her hips'
How I loved to watch them sway;
She'd grab a partner in each hand,
Allemande and then sashay;
Underneath that velvet cowboy hat
Much to my surprise,
The tired waitress stare was gone,
There was fire in those eyes!
And she kept those people dancing
Til it was time to close,
If the band had kept up to her

She'd still be dancing, Heaven knows!

She forgot that she was crazy,
She forgot about her day;
As the fiddle and the steel guitar
Moved that restaurant far away.

So now I'm shifting gears again
Across the country side;
My foot moves from the brake to clutch
With a smooth electric slide;
I think about that late night load
And that one light little town;
And how I waited for my turn
Til the teacher spun me round;
I know she's serving coffee
With one eye on the clock,
Soon that Cinderella waitress
Will turn the restaurant lock.

When the traffic drives me crazy
And I've parked it for the day,
I just find a line dance teacher
And a Country Cabaret!

Copyright Jim McGregor
Sept. 1994

DAWN

Dawn has broken with a bright shimmering glow
And your smile captivates me in that golden flow
I see within the deep recess of your eyes
A sparkle and warmth that holds no goodbyes

Your breasts rise with each breath you take
And all for wanting you my body does ache
I touch the softness beneath the sheets
Your racing heart thus counts the beats

The light of the moon caresses your body
You reach out to me and your smile is naughty
Moving closer we once again embrace
As you move my mind to a heavenly place

Never more to wake alone
With only hope upon your mind
Now in your arms the happiness you hoped to find
Trust me my beloved, and fear not a night alone
I am here and now make you my own

By Terrence Morrissey
Copyright 2009

DESTINY

You, my beloved, who dwell in the
secret recesses of my heart
How I rejoice in the day your mother gave birth to you
You were destined to be mine from the
moment you were conceived
But time and chance came and robbed me of your love

Our God has redeemed the time and
now your heart belongs to me
I belong to my beloved and she belongs to me
Your lips are sweeter than the sweetest
wine and as gentle as satin to touch
Come my beloved, lie in my arms
and let me caress your breasts

In the darkness and at twilight I will give you my love
You will tell me that you love me and
I will lift you to the heavens
I will lead you ever so gently to that place
where ecstasy meets paradise
And you will forever dwell in the
secret recesses of my love

You are beautiful, my darling, lovely as a
dew drop in the early morning sun
Your eyes open at the dawning of the morn
as a flower opens to greet the day
They seek me out as does your lips and I see
in your eyes the longing that is there
I reach out to embrace you and rest
my head on your breast

You sigh as we embrace and I hear
you whisper, 'I love you'
And there in the early morning, as the
birds begin to sing, destiny is fulfilled
As our lips meet I once again rejoice
in the day you were conceived
And my heart says a silent prayer to
God, thanking him for your birth
And I Love you just because you're you

By Terrence Morrissey
Copyright 2009

FATE AND THE HEART

Where thou hast walked fate did dwell
I drank of thine beauty as at a well
My thirst for thee at first unquenchable
Was at last made calm as fate would allow

Caressing with trembling fingers thy skin so fair
Alas aroused by fingers through thine hair
Sensing thy body alive with desire
Was in my heart a burning fire

Thee spoke of many things that night
Love was triumphant and all seemed right
To give to thee my love and life
Will fate and the heart make thee my wife?

Terrence Morrissey
Copyright 2009

FILLING UP WITH LOVE

There are those that can tell you how long it takes;

To fill a mother's heart with love,
Just the second her baby is born
Or
Fill a father's heart with pride,
Just as long as it takes to say, "It's a boy."
Or
Fill a child with heart stopping excitement,
Just when he hugs a puppy for the first time
Or
Fill a little boy's heart with gladness,
Just when his dad says, "I'm proud of you son."
Or
Fill a young lady's heart with overwhelming joy,
Just when that special guy says, "will you marry me?'
Or
Fill a young man's heart with perfect happiness,
Just when she says, "Yes!"

But only I can tell you how long it took
To fill my heart to overflowing with love

Just a moment out of a lifetime
When first you caught my eye,
smiled, and said, "Hello."

By Terrence Morrissey
Copyright 2009

FLOWERS GENTLE BENEATH OUR FEET*

What has happened to my beloved?
In the morn you were no more
What has happened to my beloved?
I asked with a sigh and a broken heart

It is all so new and all so very strange
When once I glanced you were always there
Always you were part of me,
Lo these many, many years

What has happened to my beloved?
Is written in pain across my heart
In the early morning you were no more
And in the twilight as in the early morn

What has happened to my beloved?
Perplexing as it may seem
I know you are no more upon this earth
Yet you dwell daily within my heart

Alas, I no more ask, what has happened to my beloved
For my heart now knows peace and calmness
You have gone ahead as you always have
To prepare a place for our love to bloom, forever

One day, my beloved, in God's perfect time
I will walk again with you, your hand in mine
Eternally strolling across meadows so grand
With the fragrance of flowers gentle beneath our feet

By Terrence Morrissey
Copyright 2011

*On the occasion of a friend who one day exclaimed, with a heart broken, "I miss my Florine." His wife of over fifty years had been dead for six years. I wrote this for him and it hung in his bedroom, he told me he read it every day.

FOR THE LOVE OF YOU

For the love of beautiful You
I would move the mountains into the sea
I would toss a rainbow across the sky
I would halt the storms that cause you unrest

I would capture the first flower of springtime
And gently place it upon your breast
The morning mist would frame your smile
And your laughter would fill my heart

Your laughter is as enchanting as the song of an angel
And your smile as captivating as the first fall of snow
Memories of your beauty haunt me
as I dream a dream of love
And although I love in vain, I awake each morn
For the love of you

Terrence Morrissey
Copyright 2011

FROM WHENCE DID THIS LOVE SPRING

Was it the way you took my hand
And held it with love in yours?

Was it the way you looked at me
With your beautiful and loving eyes?

Was it the way you cuddled up close and secure
As we sat beneath a tree on a moonlit night?

Was it the when you touched your cheek to mine
As I held you in my arms and we
waltzed as the music played?

Was it the thrill, joy and happiness that my heart felt?
When you laughed and angels danced in your eyes?

Was it watching you look over your
shoulder down by the lake?
When, with a trembling heart, I handed you my life?

Was it the pride I felt as you shared
share your happiness with me
When you boldly proclaimed your love for me?

No, my beloved, it was none of these
that sealed my love for you

It was a gentle kiss on a moonlit night
Whence met our lips and I heard
a thousand Angels sing

God placed the love in my heart for you, my beloved
And there it stays for all eternity

Terrence Morrissey
Copyright 2011

HAPPINESS

A TRUE AND LASTING HAPPINESS
IS ATTAINABLE

IF

YOU FIRST MAKE SURE
THAT YOUR LOVER IS HAPPY

THIS IS ESSENTIAL

FOR YOU TO GATHER TO YOURSELF
A TRUE AND LASTING HAPPINESS

Terrence Morrissey
Copyright 2011

HOW CAN I SAY I LOVE YOU

I can say it in a song
Or with a bouquet of flowers
Or dinner in really nice restaurant
Or a special gift on a special day

But anyone can say I love you
In that old fashioned way
I mean I really love you
And I want you to know how much

So I think I will just love you
For all eternity and here is what I'll do
I will tell you that I love you
By all the things I do

I will be respectful and helpful too
I will always speak well of you no matter what
I will hold your hand when you are troubled
And I will always protect you no matter what

You can count on me to be where you need me to be
I will listen with patience when you have a need to talk
I will hold you close when pain has entered your heart
But most of all I will always just say
"I love you" no matter what

Terrence Morrissey
Copyright 2009

HOW MUCH LOVE CAN
ONE HEART HOLD?

IF ALL THE LOVE THAT I HAVE FOR YOU

WAS TO BE EMPTIED INTO THE
OCEAN AND THE SEA

THEN EVERY OCEAN AND SEA IN THE WORLD

WOULD OVERFLOW ITS BANKS

Terrence Morrissey
July 2011

I LOVE YOU

BECAUSE YOU ARE SO VERY BEAUTIFUL
AND YOU FILL MY HEART WITH HAPPINESS
EVERY MINUTE OF EVERY DAY
BUT MOST OF ALL
I LOVE YOU JUST BECAUSE YOU'RE YOU

By Terrence Morrissey
Copyright 2009

I MISS MY LITTLE SISTER*

What fun we had as little girls
Frolicking in the playground with scattered curls
Laughter and joy filled our very being
I miss my little sister

Then one day we were all grown up
Serious stuff about hurts and love
A little nagging here and there
I miss my little sister

Into adulthood with problems galore
We trod together down life's path
But the laughter was gone and so were you
I miss my little sister

But just hold on a minute all you there
I know where she has gone, I certainly do
To visit with God up in the sky
I still miss my little sister

Now it all becomes clear as you will see
My sister has gone ahead, as she always has
To talk with God about you and me
I still miss my little sister

One day soon, tussled curls and all
We'll talk of happier days gone by
No more tears, nor pain nor hurt
I still miss my little sister

But not the same way anymore
The pain is less and my hurt is gone
I saw you that day as I saw the light
I still miss my little sister but now
with a heart of with joy

Terrence Morrissey
March 31, 2010

*On the occasion when a friend told me how much she missed her little sister who had died some fifteen years earlier.

I'M SMITTIN'

So, you think I'm smitten'
With a pretty kitten
Well, I'll tell you
It's darn well fittin'

For by the love bug I've been bitten
And on my rear I'm not sittin'
Or wasting my time with nothin' but knittin'
'Cause on that gal I sure am hittin'

After her heart I'm a gittin'
And I'll tell you now, I ain't quittin'
'Til by the love bug she too is bitten
And by the fire we'll both be sittin'

Terrence Morrissey
Copyright 2009

IN THE SHADOW OF THE
SETTING SUN*

One night I saw you out walking,
Oh what a pretty sight you were
As you walked in the shadow of the setting sun
Your little granddaughter, holding tightly to your hand

Did you think of days not so long ago?
When on an evening very much like this
You held the hand of your own dear daughter
And walked with her in the shadow of a setting sun

And sometime, in the future not so far away
Your little granddaughter will also one day walk
In the Shadow of a mighty setting sun,
holding her daughter's hand
When destiny walks hand in hand
In God's almighty plan

Terrence Morrissey
Copyright 2009

*One evening, as the sun was setting, I was looking out my window and my neighbor walked by holding her granddaughter's hand.

INFINITE TRUST
(A Beautiful Sentiment)

I always had infinite trust in him over
the decisions he made for us

Because I realized that often my heart
would overrule my head.

He kept us on a solid footing

By Muriel Arnason upon her husband's death, after 56
years of marriage, June 25th 2005

Included in this book with deep gratitude.

Terrence Morrissey
August 23, 2011

JUST A FEW FLOWERS

I know of the pain that fills your heart
It robs you of the joys the world would offer
Never, it seems, will it disappear
Always there, forever stealing joy and peace

But wait, there is a way, or so it seems
To bring back that joy and peace
that are rightfully yours
I call it the ladder of optimism and
it's at the door of your heart
Knocking ever so gently and always with a smile

So up the ladder we go, step by step
glancing upward all the while
Forever keeping your eye on the goal above
Now you have reached the top and
etched in a cloud are these words
God, will help you, to accept the
things you cannot change

Let your heart be at peace and let the joy flood in
For your God has given you the power
to change only the things you can
The rest is left to Him, and it is His
plan that will be fulfilled
God sends you flowers to help you know
that it is His Hand upon your heart

That will bring back your peace and joy
A dozen roses, each filled with love,
to soothe your aching heart
Smell the fragrance of peace and the fragrance of joy
And feel the closeness of God

Terrence Morrissey
Copyright 2009

LOVE BEFORE A SONG

I AWOKE THIS MORNING OUT OF A DEEP SLEEP
BEFORE THE BIRDS BEGAN THEIR
EARLY MORNING TRILL
MY HEART WOULD NOT BE STILL
NOT EVEN FOR A MOMENT
MY BEATING HEART STARTLED EVEN
THE SILENCE OF THE MORN

AS A DEW DROP NEEDS AN
EARLY MORNING ROSE
AND AS A FISH NEEDS A MOVING
SPARKLING RIVER
AS A BIRD ON THE WING NEEDS
A GENTLY SWAYING WIND
SO DOES MY HEART NEED GOD
FOR IT TO BEGIN TO SING

Terrence Morrissey
Copyright 9/3/2008

MY BELOVED

My beloved has stolen my heart
But not stolen really, for I give it willingly
Her caress has captured my imagination
But not captured really, for I imagine freely

The touch of her body has ensnared my senses
And I am a slave, body heart and soul
But not a slave really, for I am enslaved by ecstasy
As I envision her strolling into my room

The smile of love captures me once again
And I succumb to the touch of
her hand across my body
Giving so tenderly of her love, she is mine
And I scarce can breathe for the love that engulfs me

Terrence Morrissey
Copyright 2009

MY BELOVED, MY PIANO AND ME

The room was large like an enormous ballroom
The walls were white, a beautiful angelic white
The sun filtered with brilliance through lace curtains,
As comforting shadows swayed gently to the music

My beloved's favorite song softly filled the air
And was mellow beneath my ever moving finger tips
As I caressed the smooth white ivory of the piano
A teardrop on my cheek, I was
sure that she had smiled

My love of fifty years or more lay still upon her bed
Her eyes were closed and her countenance sweet
And the beauty of yesteryear was calm upon her face
Did she hear the music, I reflected as I played

They came shortly thereafter, those
folks all dressed in white
And wheeled her bed across that
immense hospital room
Out the swinging doors she went
not conscious of a thing
I played on until the dusk, and then
closed the piano down

Walking through those swinging
doors I heard an angel say
Wipe the tear from your eye for today
she really heard you play

In the future, not so far away, I will
once again hear her laughter
But for the present all alone I sit
and play her favorite song

They buried my beloved today and as the silence rang
I could hear the angels singing as
she danced among the clouds
A smile upon her face as she waits for
me to play her favorite song,
Alone together once more, my
beloved, my piano and me

For my good friend Doug Armstrong reminiscing about the last days of his dear wife. Thank you for your friendship and allowing me to put your feelings into words.

Terrence Morrissey
Copyright June 6, 2011

MY LAST TRUE LOVE

Was it the sinking crimson sun beyond the horizon?
Or was it the last flower of summer
Possibly it was the sigh of a baby
As it drifted off to sleep

Maybe it the last sight of a waterfall
As the morning mist engulfed it
Could it be the beauty of a full golden moon?
As it first peeked above the horizon

Just maybe, it was the first flower of springtime
Opening alone upon a mountain top
Or possibly the early morning laughter of a baby
Discovering its toes for the first time

It surely must have been the cascading water
As the early morning dams are opened
As I contemplate the sinking sun beyond the horizon
And the last flower of summer

Hearing softly the sigh of a baby drifting off to sleep
And a misty morning waterfall
I see clearly the majesty of a full golden moon
And the blossoming of spring's first flower

Now it is the cascading water
As the flood gates are opened that I think upon
And putting all this together I am mindful
Of my love for you when first we met

The flower did bloom, the water did flow,
The sun peeked over the horizon and a baby laughed
And then I thought of the sunset of my life
And the last flower of my summer

Which of these would I choose to gaze upon?
Before being lifted to eternity
I can have them all by seeing, at my last,
Your sweet face before me, for you shall be
MY LAST TRUE LOVE

Terrence Morrissey
Copyright 2009

OBSESSION

I wonder what kind of perfume she wears.
I'd like to get a small bottle to keep;
I'd sprinkle a few little drops on my pillow
So she would be in my dreams when I sleep.

I'd spray just a little on my shoulder or sleeve
So I could pretend she was standing right there;
Then fantasize that she was talking and laughing,
Casually brushing my cheek with her hair.

I could take some to work, and, there in my office,
Just dab a small bit on my phone,
Then the rest of the day I'd put people on hold
And be with her all alone.

That fragrance I know is some Voodoo potion,
Designed to catch me off guard, unawares;
Then my whole day is spent, in search of that scent,
Wondering what kind of perfume she wears!

J.S. McGregor

ONCE UPON A TIME

HIGH UPON A MOUNTAIN TOP THERE APPEARED A GOLDEN FLOWER PLACED THERE EVER SO GENTLY BY THE VERY HAND OF GODTHE FLOWER WAS YOUNG AND BROUGHT A SMILE AS A GIFT TO THE ENTIRE WORLD.BUT ALAS, LONESOMENESS BROUGHT A FROWN ONE DAY AND MADE THE GOLDEN FLOWER SO SAD

BUT GOD, IN ALL HIS LOVE, PLACED A MAN TO MAKE THINGS BRIGHT "BE VERY CAREFUL" GOD HAD SAID, "FOR THIS GOLDEN FLOWER IS FRAGILE" DON'T HARM THE GOLDEN FLOWER OR MAKE HER CRY OR WEEP FOR SHE IS VERY SPECIAL TO ME AND I WATCH HER EVEN WHEN SHE SLEEPS. THE MAN WAS HAPPY THAT HE HAD BEEN PLACED NEXT TO THIS PRECIOUS FLOWER, FOR HE TOO WAS LONELY AND NEEDED LOVE AND SO HE DID ALL THAT HE THOUGHT WAS RIGHT.

THEN ONE DAY THE GOLDEN FLOWER LOST ITS LUSTER AND THE SMILE DID DISAPPEAR "WHAT HAS HAPPENED?" GOD ASKED ONE DAY, HIS HEART ANGUISHED AT WHAT HE SAW. "I DON'T KNOW," THE MAN DID ANSWER, "I DID ALL THAT I THOUGHT WAS RIGHT." THE LITTLE FLOWER, WITH A TEAR DROP IN HER EYE, DID LOOK TO GOD FOR COMFORT AND PINED TO HAVE HER SMILE RETURNED.

"WAIT", SAID THE GENTLE MAN, AS HE CONTEMPLATED ALL THESE THINGS, "I

HAVE MADE A SERIOUS MISTAKE AND NEVER REALIZED WHAT I DID. I AM THE ONE THAT HAS STOLEN THE GOLDEN LUSTER AND ROBBED HER OF HER SMILE." I SEE NOW THE ERROR OF MY WAYS AND ASK TO BE FORGIVEN. I KNOW THAT LOVE AND GENTLENESS AND KINDNESS ARE THE THINGS THAT MADE THE GOLDEN FLOWER SHINE AND PEACE AND SWEETNESS PUT A SMILE ON HER FACE AND I HAVE TAKEN THAT AWAY. FROM THIS MOMENT ON, I WILL MEND MY WAYS AND BRING THE LUSTER BACK TO THE GOLDEN FLOWER AND MY LOVE WILL BE SUCH THAT HER SMILE WILL RETURN NEVER TO BE LOST AGAIN.

GOD WAS HAPPY TO HEAR THESE WORDS AS WAS THE GOLDEN FLOWER AND THEY FORGAVE THE MAN BECAUSE HIS HEART WAS SINCERE AND ANOTHER CHANCE WAS HIS. THE GOLDEN FLOWER, TURNED INTO A BEAUTIFUL BALLERINA AND SHONE JUST LIKE THE SUN. SHE DANCED ACROSS THE BILLOWY CLOUDS AND BROUGHT HAPPINESS TO EVERYONE.

GOD LOOKED DOWN, A SMILE HIS FACE DID SHOW, AND AS HE CONTEMPLATED ALL THESE THINGS HE KNEW THAT THE MAN AND HIS LITTLE GOLDEN GIRL WOULD LOVE ONE ANOTHER FOREVER.

BUT WHAT NAME SHALL YOU CALL THE GIRL, YOUR ONE AND ONLY GOLDEN FLOWER; THE ANGELS DID ASK ONE DAY? "WHAT ELSE WOULD I CALL HER," SAID GOD. "SHE IS LIKE A BEAUTIFUL SPRING DAY, I WILL CALL HER 'HEAVEN'S GIFT' AND SHE WILL FILL THE MAN

WITH GLADNESS AND HE IN TURN WILL LOVE
HER UNTIL HIS DYING DAY. "

Terrence Morrissey
Copyright 2009

ONE SOLITARY LIFE

Here is a man who was born in an obscure village, a child of a peasant woman. He grew up in another village. He worked in a carpenter shop until he was thirty. Then for three years he was an itinerant preacher

He never owned a home. He never wrote a book. He never held an office. He never had a family. He never went to college. He never put his foot inside a big city. He never traveled two hundred miles from the place He was born. He never did one of the things that usually accompany greatness. He had no credentials but himself ....

While still a young man, the tide of popular opinion turned against him. His friends ran away. One of them denied Him. He was turned over to his enemies. He went through the mockery of a trial. He was nailed on a cross between two thieves. While he was dying his executioners gambled for the only piece of property he had on earth -- his coat. When he was dead, he was laid in a borrowed grave through the pity of a friend.

Twenty long centuries have come and gone, and today He is the centerpiece of the human race and leader of the column of progress.

I am far within the mark when I say that all the armies that ever marched, all the navies that were ever built; all parliaments that ever sat and all the kings that ever ruled, put together, have not affected the life of man upon this earth as powerfully as that one solitary life.

This year, for the Two Thousand and Eleventh time, I celebrate, and I hope you do also, the birthday of Jesus whom some call a prophet, some call just another man but two billion persons call Him what He is….the Son of a living, loving God.

Author Unknown*

Terrence Morrissey
June 7, 2011

ONE SUNLIT MORN

My heart took flight one early morn
And soared across a sky so grand
Touching clouds and angels too
All because you smiled at me one sunlit morn

Never would I leave you, no never would I go
For my heart belongs to you alone
That love was gifted by God above
All because you smiled at me one sunlit morn

Sail on, sail on my heart doth cry
Touch the clouds and angels too
As you soar across a sky so grand
All because you smiled at me one sunlit morn

Terrence Morrissey
Copyright 2009

PERFECT LOVE*

Love is patient, love is kind
It does not envy, it does not boast
It is not proud, it is not rude
It is not self seeking
It is not easily angered
It keeps no record of wrongs
Love does not delight in evil
But rejoices with the truth
It always protects, always trusts,
Always hopes, always perseveres
Love never fails

*NIV Scofield Study Bible 1st Corinthians Chapter 13
Verses 4-8

PINK SHOES

I first heard the gentle steps approaching from behind
Turning I looked down and that
was when I first saw her
A gracious and pleasant smile standing in
The Pink Shoes

How cute, I thought as my eyes wandered
First the ankles, how tiny and smooth they were
And then long slim legs, but my eyes wandered back to
The Pink Shoes

A voice as sweet as honeycomb spoke gently
Hi, she spoke, and her emerald blue eyes
Danced a flirting dance as I looked once again at
The Pink shoes

Strawberry blonde hair caught in a gentle breeze
As she looked out from behind a veil of softness
I could scarcely breathe as I beheld the beauty of
The Pink Shoes

I am perplexed as I contemplate
Why would anyone wear pink shoes?
To take out the trash?

Terrence Morrissey

POETRY AND LOVE

Poetry is not written about love

But rather about the memory of love

Of loving and being loved

Of hearing a songbird at twilight

Of melting into a lover's arms

CAPTURING, IN A HEARTBEAT

The most beautiful part of love

That intimate moment

When love meets love

And memories are forever made

By Terrence Morrissey
Copyright 2011

SEEING YOU WITHOUT ME

SEEING YOU WITHOUT ME
WOULD BE LIKE SEEING A SUNRISE
WITHOUT THE SUN
OR A GOLDEN SUNSET WITHOUT THE GOLD
OR A BLUE SKY WITHOUT THE BLUE

SEEING YOU WITHOUT ME
WOULD BE LIKE SEEING THE
END OF A RAINFALL
WITHOUT A RAINBOW
OR THE END OF A DAY WITHOUT
THE TWILIGHT

SEEING YOU WITHOUT ME
WOULD BE LIKE SEEING A
MOUNTAIN BUT NOT THE TOP
OR THE SEA WITHOUT WATER
OR THE OCEAN WITHOUT FISH

SEEING YOU WITHOUT ME
WOULD BE LIKE SEEING A BEAUTIFUL BEACH
WITHOUT A PALM TREE
OR A SLEEPING BEAUTY WITHOUT SEEING YOU

SEEING YOU WITHOUT ME
WOULD BE LIKE SEEING A DREAM WALKING
AND YOU WOULD BE MISSING
OR SEEING AN ANGEL WITHOUT
SEEING HEAVEN

SEEING YOU WITHOUT ME WOULD BE LIKE
SEEING MY HEART BROKEN IN
A THOUSAND PIECES

By Terrence Morrissey
Copyright 2009

SLEEP WALKING

Most of her left leg from her thigh to her ankle
Is uncovered;
The smoothness of her skin contrasts with the tossed
And tumbled creases in the sheets;
It is dark except for a sliver of streetlight
That has peeked in,
Through where the drapes
Are hanging crookedly,
Waiting for the hook to be replaced;
The light sets a gentle halo on her hair
That has spilled and scattered
Across the whiteness of the pillow;
It is just enough light that I can see
The freckles on her shoulder,
And the Christmas earrings she almost never takes off;
Her eyelids hide her eyes and yet,
Their movement reveals a dream dancing inside,
And I can only hope I am some small part of it;
Her lips are not quite smiling, but
I can still taste them from where I stand,
And feel the tremble their touch brings,
And taste the tears that come after their whispers;
It is cold and my housecoat is on
a hook behind the door,
If I reach for it, it may break the spell;
If I thought for a second I deserved her,
I would go back to bed, and risk waking her,
But God, I could stand here for
hours, watching her sleep.

J.S. McGregor

SWEET LAUGHTER

All earth's creatures are stilled

And a million angels begin to sing

For out of the abundance of your heart

Comes the sound of sweetness

And all of Heaven rejoices

Terrence Morrissey
Copyright 2009

THE DAY YOU WENT AWAY

As the dawn breaks,
Forcing aside the last shadows of the night
I awake in silence and in tears
As in days forever past and in days yet to come
Like a ghost I tread a weary path
Where the flowers have no fragrance
And the sun never shines
Music does not my soul make happy
Never, since the day you went away

The smile upon my face is forever gone
Yet.... what sound falls upon my ear
It is but the sound of silence and of tears
As night falls and I lay down my weary head
My body feels not the sensation of life
Prayer reaches out to the ghosts of yesteryear
Imploring and beseeching that not again tomorrow
Will dawn break in silence and in tears
As since the day you went away

Terrence Morrissey
Copyright 2009

THE HARBOUR OF MY HEART

The sails of my beloved, blowing in the breeze
At last anchored in the Harbour of my heart
From whence you came, I know not
You were there since time began, a destiny fulfilled

When on the tide you sailed away
You took with you, the treasure
I had buried deep within
The treasure was your love for me

As the dawn breaks upon the morn'
I search the horizon with an aching heart
Shall I see those sails at last appear?
Or shall there forever be an empty
Harbour in my heart

Terrence Morrissey

THE ALCOHOLIC AND THE HUG

I walked into the room one miserable day
And I heard some people say hey,
it's good to see you today
Grab a chair and a coffee too, we'd like you to stay
With coffee in hand I stayed out of their way

Well I sat in the corner and kept an eye on them all
They talked about good times and bad times too
But mostly they talked about the day they first arrived
It saved my life, one was heard to say
and mine too another one spoke

Ok, so what's the secret I was thinking to myself
That made them so darn happy that
their laughter filled the hall
Half dead on Monday and alive on
Tuesday, it just didn't make sense
I went back out another one said, well
welcome back was the chorus I heard

And on it went for almost an hour with
lots of laughs and a few tears too
But tears seemed to strengthen the lot as they
joked about this and joked about that
By golly I said to myself at the end, this
is the place to find a good friend
I stood to go and they did too but I
couldn't get out without a hug or two

Keep coming back were the words that I
heard and sincere it was of that I was sure
I'll come back, I said with surprise because
today I met the cure for my disease
I'll live another day I thought as I grinned
and made my way out the door
It was the hug that did it and I knew it for sure,
I'll be back for more I said with a smile

Terrence Morrissey
July 2011

THE KISS

I SAW A RAIBOW IN THE SKY
I FELT A GENTLE BREEZE UPON MY LIPS
THE FEELING OF SOFTNESS THAT I FELT
WAS AS A BUTTERFLY SETTLING UPON A ROSE
AND I KNEW THAT YOUR LIPS
HAD TOUCHED MINE

Terrence Morrissey
Copyright 2009

THE MORNING DAWN

I call her dawn and just like the dawn of the morn'
She awakes each day aglow with laughter
Happiness as bright as sunshine flows from her
As she gathers her tresses round 'bout her

Watching beguiled as she glides softly across the room
Golden sunlight sweeping ever so
gently across her body
Laughter fills the room as she tilts her lovely face
And claims a new day has broken for she is my dawn

Terrence Morrissey
August 2011

THE NIGHT THE BIRDS SANG

In the stillness of a quiet night
About the midnight hour, as my beloved slept
A tranquil and angelic smile all
at once adorned her face
A smile so lovely that its radiance awoke even the birds
Who were sleeping a deep and mellow sleep
It was the night the birds began to sing
At a time they had never sung before
They sang a song of love to my beloved

By Terrence Morrissey
Copyright 2009

THE VOICE OF AN ANGEL

In a dreamlike trance I heard an angel speak
Softly, gently, beguiling and inviting
My heart stopped, or so it seemed
Suddenly I heard a host of angels singing

What manner of heaven is this spoke my heart
For I am bewitched, enchanted and captivated
A sound so sweet that even the birds stopped singing
And paid rapturous attention to a voice so lovely

In an instant I awoke and looking around me
I realized that I had been bewitched and charmed
By the voice of an angel speaking a heavenly language
With a voice like a gentle summer's breeze

Terrence Morrissey

THE WAVE UPON THE SHORE

LYING NAKED BENEATH A SHIMMERING MOON
THE NAKED LADY SIGHED
AS A MEMORY TOUCHED HER MIND
FOR NOT SO MANY YEARS AGO

IN A PLACE SUCH AS THIS
HER LOVER TOOK HER IN HIS ARMS
THEIR BODIES EMBRACED WITH A LOVE
THAT PROMISED TO NEVER END

A FEELING OF SOARING ABOVE HERSELF
AND LOOKING DOWN AS A THOUSAND DAYS
FLEETINGLY PASSED BEFORE HER VERY EYES
LET THIS NEVER END THE
NAKED LADY DID SIGH

THE WARMTH OF A WAVE GENTLY
TOUCHED HER TOES
AS THE OCEAN BEGAN ITS RITUAL CRAWL
ACROSS A THOUSAND OCEANS
AND UP UPON THE LAND
SLOWLY, EVER SLOWLY, GENTLY
EVER SO GENTLY

SHE WAS ONCE AGAIN
EMBRACED BY HER LOVER
THE NAKED LADY AWAKENED
AND WITH A SIGH THAT HUSHED THE NIGHT
THE NAKED LADY KNEW

THAT THE DREAM SHE DREAMED
SHE WOULD DREAM NO MORE
FOR HER LOVER WAS ONLY
THE WAVE UPON THE SHORE

By Terrence Morrissey
Copyright 2009

THEY DON'T KNOW HOW

They don't know how not to hurt
They don't know how to stop the pain
They don't know how not to kill
They don't know how not to suffer

How does a man know how not to kill?
When his whole life he is taught to hate.
How does a boy know not to steal?
When his whole life he has been hungry.

How does a woman know how not to give birth?
When her whole life she has been told it's right.
How does a man know how not to suffer?
When he has never had the tools to ease the pain.

How does a world fall into silence?
When a million fellow humans are slaughtered.
How does the one at the top view
suffering without feeling?
When he has been taught that money is his god.

How does mankind do all these things?
When he has been taught that God is dead.
How does his conscience not instruct him otherwise?
How you well might ask?
When he is no longer answerable to a higher power.

By Terrence Morrissey
Copyright 2009

TRUE LOVE

The wonderful love of a beautiful babe

The love of a staunch true man

The love of a baby unafraid

Has existed since life began

But the greatest love

The love of loves

Even greater than that of a mother

Is the infinite, tender and passionate love

That we share …. one for another.

*An adaption
Author Unknown

Terrence Morrissey.
July 2011

TWILIGHT

It was twilight when I first heard the song
Sweet sounding and gentle to my ear
The beauty of the song caressed my heart
And I saw your loveliness deep within that song

It was twilight and the sun was
fading into a western sky
Crimson red with hues of blue and
amber touching the evening sky
I saw you smile in the twilight as a
restful breeze caressed your lips
My heart wept a tear of joy as I thought
of the twilight of our love

Deep within this heart of mine a
caressing love was sown
And gently began to bloom the first
petals of love's sweet song
I feel your embrace as the twilight
embraces the evening
Crimson red with hues of blue and
amber touching the evening sky

Terrence Morrissey
Copyright 2009

WAKE ME NOT

Your smile plays a melody of love across my heart
Your eyes hold my heart captive for eternity
Your laughter makes music where
no music has existed
Your beauty and charm captivate me

So play on and on and on, never ending
A song of love, a melody of enchantment
Make music with your laughter
Captivate me for eternity with your beauty

A misty moonlight, a walk in the sand
All the angels in heaven are singing
A song of love so grand
And into my arms you stroll

Stay another minute, linger a moment more
Let me hold you as you play a melody of love
Across my heart with your smile so captivating
I am captive, held for eternity, wake me not

Terrence Morrissey
Copyright 2009

WALKING THE HIGHWAYS
AND THE BYWAYS

With a broken heart, I'm walking
The highways and the byways
Under a cloudy sky

The birds have stilled their song
The people have lost their smile
And a dog bit me on my rear

A dog peed upon my shoe
A bird pooped on my head
And a snake crawled up my leg

Is this any way to treat a man
Who is walking the Highways and the Byways
With a broken heart?

Terrence Morrissey
Copyright 2009

WHAT I SAW

You asked me what I saw
When I looked across the room,
An angel peeking out from beneath a halo
And Thunder crashing within my heart

Surely heaven is missing an angel thought I
As I begged my heart be still
An angel dancing on a silver cloud
As one dancing in a dream

Then my heart was silent as silent as the night
Beneath the misty moonlight across a crowded room
Danced heavenly beauty enshrined
in a captivating smile
A heavenly vision is what I really saw

Terrence Morrissey
Copyright 2009

WHERE HAVE YOU GONE?

YOUR HEART, LIKE A ROSE
I HELD GENTLY TO MY BREAST
YOUR SMILE, BRIGHT AS A DIAMOND
GLISTENED AS A DEW DROP ON A PETAL
IN THE EARLY MORNING MIST

THEN ONE DAY YOU WERE GONE
AND A TEAR DROP FELL FROM MY HEART
AS THE LAST ROSE OF SUMMER GAVE WAY
TO THE EARLY MORNING FROST OF FALL
AND YOU WERE NO MORE

Terrence Morrissey
Copyright 2009

WHISPERING EYES

When I look into your eyes
I see not love but bewilderment
I see the pain of a thousand yesterdays
Trust is gone, in its place there is hesitation

Oh, if only you could understand
How you have moved me, mind body and soul
To love you with a love that no man can measure
I long for you to embrace my love

Your pain of yesterday has become my pain of today
I long to see the love in your eyes embrace me
As I have never been embraced before
Hold me to your breast and trust in my love

The nights are short as you lay in my arms
Too short and I beg them to last forever
Let me hold you, my teary eyed beauty
And wipe away those tears of yesterday

My arms are strong
My resolve stronger still
To protect you and love you
As you have never been loved before

Soon your eyes will sparkle like the morning dew
I will hear you sigh a sigh of contented love
In the early morn as the birds begin to sing
Your eyes will sing ever so softly a song of love

By Terrence Morrissey
Copyright 2009

WHO ELSE

Who gave the birds their songs to sing?
Who wrote the words, who wrote the melody?
Who put the thrill in the trill as the little bird sang?
Who, you might ask with acceptable awe

Who made the grass, you well may ask?
Who designed the individual blade?
Who made the carpet across the meadow?
Who, you might ask with acceptable awe

Who made the flower, who created
the million designs?
Who brought those colors together?
Who ever heard of making a blade of grass?
Who, you might ask with acceptable awe

Who put the rainbow in the sky?
Who designed the colors?
Who placed it so the whole world would see?
Who, you might ask with acceptable awe

Who ever heard of giving songs to the birds?
Who ever heard of placing rainbows on high?
Who else I would answer, who but He
The one and only, who else but God

Copyright 2009 by:
Terrence Morrissey
Music By Deenie

YOUR EYES

YOUR EYES SPARKLE
AS A DEW DROP SPARKLES ON A ROSE,
IN THE EARLY MORNING MIST

WHEN YOU SMILE AT THE BREAK OF DAWN
AND THE BIRDS BEGIN TO SING
ALL OF GOD'S CREATION IS STILLED

A THOUSAND ANGELS HERALD THE DAY
AND ALL OVER THE WORLD
A MILLION FLOWERS BEGIN TO BLOOM

ALL OF THIS IN THE EARLY MORNING MIST
JUST BECAUSE OF THE SMILE ON YOUR FACE
AND THE SPARKLE IN YOUR EYES

Terrence Morrissey
Copyright 2009

YOUR HAND IN MINE

Your hand was meant to be held in mine
When we walk at twilight beside a lake
And a golden moonbeam dances across the water
And a shower of gold caresses your smile

Your hand was meant to be held in mine
When we walk and talk on a city street
Holding tight as the crowds push by
And horns will blare as cars rush by

Your hand was meant to caress my brow
On an evening when day is done
When unsettled and weary my heart shall fail
And you touch my mind as you touch my face

Your hand, the hand of a gentle woman
Speaks to my heart without a sound
When once you look up into my eyes
I know your hand was meant to be held in mine

Terrence Morrissey
Copyright 2009

THE OBEDIENCE FACTOR

ABOUT THE AUTHOR

This short story you are about to read is absolutely true in every way. It is one man's account of an unselfish act that set a chain of events into motion. It is not an epic tale of heroism or the chronicle of the defeat of an army. It begins when he simply gives away his last $5.00 and tells us how the sowing of that seed reaped him a harvest of $150.000.00.

It reinforces the lesson that 'what we sow, so shall we reap' and that God's laws and nature's laws will never fail. Once again, we are reminded, money is neither the beginning nor the end of all happiness.

Having spent about twenty three years of his life as an alcoholic, from the age of fourteen to the age of thirty seven, Terrence lived the life of an out of control drinker. All of the decisions and problems that come with being an alcoholic he has experienced.

Terrence has lived in the Bahamas, Puerto Rico, the Virgin Islands, California and Hawaii for most of his working life and sadness followed him everywhere. Until one day while walking down Kalakaua Avenue in Waikiki he had an encounter with God. The enormity of that encounter was so huge that in one split second he was delivered from a life of alcoholism and has had no desire to drink for the past thirty six years. But that is another story for another time.

Terrance tells us, "God has taught me, these past

thirty six years, all about sowing and reaping and it is my desire to pass along information about God's law that never fails. Sowing and reaping is as perfect as is the law of gravity and both never fail. Fool around with the law of gravity and you could get hurt as well as getting hurt if you fool around with God's law of sowing and reaping. I have finally learned to give and expect nothing in return, but God's law over rides my own thinking and the harvest has always come in at the exact and precise time and that timing is in the hands of God."

This story will remind you to plant your seeds of love, compassion, trust, friendship and a friendly smile and your harvest will be there when the time is ripe. This same law also applies to the sowing seeds of money.... do it with the right motive, expecting nothing in return, and God will see to your harvest.

Jim McGregor*

Terrence is available to share his amazing story with a wide variety of audiences. He is sought after as a speaker at churches, social organizations and any place that people need to be uplifted. As Terrence says about his speaking engagements, "I am not a professional speaker...I just like to help others and hopefully my story will do just that."

*Jim McGregor is a Feature Writer for the Langley Times Newspaper

DEDICATION
"The Obedience Factor"

I would like to dedicate this work to my brother Patrick Morrissey, who has shown me, over the years, what the meaning of 'true courage' and 'selfless giving' really is. Patrick, as a highly decorated veteran of the Vietnam conflict, has inspired me endlessly. Patrick's giving of himself, his love and finances left me with no end of admiration for him. "Thanks "Patrick for being a real true inspiration to me and to many, many others."

Terrence Morrissey
July 2011

THE "WOW" FACTOR
By Dr. Tom Leding

"Wow" is what came to mind the moment I read the first page of "The Obedience factor," an awesome story about the power to Jesus to redeem every facet of our lives. This is a great book that reminds me how personal God's love is for me. This compelling story grabs you from the beginning and helps you to understand what real loneliness and rejection feels like. More importantly, it puts into perspective the most important things in life, such as a relationship with God. This is a splendid example of how the hand of God can heal all wounds and boost us toward the goal of realizing our innate potential. When you finish the book, you will realize nothing is impossible with God.

Dr. Tom Leding

Dr. Leding is a leading dynamic speaker and can be seen on TV all across America and other countries. Check your local TV guide for listings under "Tom Leding Ministries." Further check out Dr. Leding's books at your local bookstore you will be more than pleasantly surprised at the positive turn your life will take when you read anyone of his 'best sellers.'

Disclaimer
It is important to note that although Dr, Leding read and was gracious enough to review "The Obedience Factor" he has not read any of the poems and therefore

his review does not include the 'Poetry Section" of this book, although I pray he would approve.

Terrence Morrissey
August 2011

THE OBEDIENCE FACTOR
(Obedience and the Harvest)

It was an unusually warm day.... in fact it was downright hot. Well, you might say, that is what Hawaii is all about.... hot days. You would be right of course, I had lived in Hawaii for about five years and hot days were nothing new to me, but this was extraordinary, the temperature at 7:15 in the morning was hovering around 92 degrees and I could see the heat as it rose from the asphalt in front of me.

I turned the corner onto Kalakaua Avenue and headed across the vast expanse of the park and into the shade of the overhanging palm trees. I was well aware of the absence of the usual, ever occurring, breezes that made living in Hawaii so comfortable. I was leaving my apartment which was located just off the Ala Wai Canal for a much needed walk in the park to cool off.

I loved living next to the "Ala Wai" which means "Freshwater Way." This is an extraordinary waterway at the western entrance to Waikiki. The 'Canal' was constructed in 1922 and drains up to 150 inches of rainwater, each year, which runs off the mountains above Waikiki. Prior to the construction and completion of the canal, the southeastern coast of Oahu was a swampland of fish and duck ponds.

After the canal was completed, the land was reclaimed and the result was the most famous tourist and beach area in the world – Waikiki. The walkway along the canal is well lit and perfect for jogging, strolling and relaxing. Most afternoons outrigger crews can be seen practicing along this beautiful waterway.

The beautiful Hawaiian Convention Centre, golf courses, apartments and condominiums line the long stretch of waterway all the way to the ocean where it empties into the Ala Wai Yacht Harbor. The Ala Wai canal marks the entrance to Waikiki and Kalakaua Avenue. Kalakaua Avenue is to my life what water is to a dying thirst craved man alone in the desert. But that is another story for another time.

I needed a walk in the park to try to cool off a little. My apartment did not have air-conditioning and was the proverbial hot box.

Spotting McDonald's restaurant on the other side of the park I headed in that direction. I would hopefully find some respite from the heat of the morning under a leafy Palm tree and then I would head over to McDonald's for a bite of breakfast. Being a bachelor McDonald's served as my kitchen away from home, with the exception that I didn't do the cooking. A nice hot egg McMuffin, hash browns and a cup of the really good tasting hot McDonald's coffee, that I loved so much, was mentally mouth watering.

Reaching into my pocket I could feel the crisp five dollar bill that I had there. It was my last five dollars as I had lost my job when the company I worked for suddenly up and locked its doors declaring bankruptcy. It took me by complete surprise and as I had just spent my last few dollars paying my rent and utilities I was left with this crisp five dollar bill until I found another job. Finding a job did not worry me to much as there were plenty of jobs available.

I had been out of work for about a week and I was now about to spend my last five dollars, or a portion of it, on my favorite breakfast, an egg McMuffin, hash brown and a cup of coffee. Foolish choice you might say and that would be true of a lot of choices I made. But I had an extremely high level of confidence and knew that I would be back at work in a few days or a week at the longest.

As I walked across the park checking out the shadiest tree I could find, for a little rest before breakfast, I noticed a huge dumpster sitting off to one side near the corner of the park. Sticking out of the dumpster was what looked like the rear end of a huge male. The legs were actively dangling and the body was hanging inside the dumpster from the waist with the chest shoulders and head completely out of site. I thought I was in bad shape, well at least I was going to have my egg McMuffin, and that poor devil was going to have whatever tid bits and left over's he could find. I felt sorry for him but what could I do, I only had a five dollar bill in my pocket and that wasn't enough to feed the both of us. On another occasion, if I was flush with money, I would not have hesitated about sharing with him. I was a Christian and tried my best to live up to that designation. Helping others was not a foreign act to me it was something that I delighted in and always felt a sense of joy when contributing to the betterment of someone else. But there is a limit to everything and my tummy was starting to rebel about the delay in feeding it.

Then it happened; I heard, what some people refer to as that still small voice, somewhere within me, saying "Give him the five dollars." But the voice was neither small nor still, it sounded more like my old drill instructor on the parade square in Cornwallis Nova Scotia when I joined the navy. "Give him the five dollars" repeated the drill instructor. I was accustomed to these orders. I took a great deal of delight from obeying the Lord. The outcome was always a joy to behold. But this time I was in a rebellious mood or should I say my stomach was rebelling against these new orders and I was inclined to agree with my tummy, the start of the rumbling in my stomach was pushing me into rebellion against that small still drill instructor type voice inside of my spirit.

"But, but, but" I started to say. I was interrupted with "No buts about it, obedience, not sacrifice is what I require."

The voice had me, I knew my bible and I knew what was required of me as a Christian. I cannot say I am one thing and then do the opposite. My loving Father in heaven knows that I fall short all too often. If I am a Christian or a Christ follower, then I have no choice but to do exactly as the bible and my God instructs even if it is contrary to what I want to do. This was absolutely contrary to what I wanted to do....I wanted an egg McMuffin, Hash browns and a cup of coffee.

"Ok" I spoke silently to that voice, "I will do as you ask and is there anything further you want me to do, should I go into the salvation message along with parting with my five dollars?"

I had being taking the message of Christ's love and death on the cross to hundreds these past few months. Preaching on the beaches in Waikiki, in parks and any other place that the Lord provided for me. I loved God, I loved Jesus and obeying the Holy Spirit was an incredible joy. The outcome of obedience far surpassed any other joy that I had ever experienced in my lifetime.

"Don't preach this time" the small voice spoke inside of me, "just give him the five dollars and say that God told you to do it and then leave."

I turned away from the huge palm tree that I was starting to settle under and headed for the rear end sticking out of the dumpster. I reached the dumpster and was face to face (so to speak) with this incredibly huge rear end covered by a pair of filthy overalls. "Excuse me sir" I said as I tapped the overalls, "I have something for you."

The overalls fell backwards out of the dumpster pound by pound. This guy was enormous, he was huge and under the top part of the overall straps, covering his chest was an old musty, food encrusted muscle shirt. I took a step backwards as he almost stumbled into my arms. I had heard the expression 'gentle giant' before but this was the first time I had ever encountered one. He was huge, he was huge all over. His arms were the size of twin cannons and his head, loaded with an incredible amount of hair, was the size of large watermelon. He was about six feet five inches tall and maybe even taller. He looked down at me with the kindest eyes I think I have ever encountered and for that I was grateful or I would probably have been a cloud of dust heading in a direction away from this encounter.

"What did you say?"
He spoke with gentleness and a kindness that really overwhelmed me.
"I said I have something for you"
I held out my hand and put the five dollar bill in his hand.
"Thanks, thanks a lot" he said.

We both stood there looking at each other, him looking down at me and me looking up, in awe, at him. "Thanks a lot" he repeated and the silence was awkward. I took a step closer to him as I handed him my last crisp five dollar bill,
"God told me to give it to you"

I felt my grasp tightening on the money...but I let go and it slipped from my hand into his. There goes breakfast I thought, oh well 'obedience over sacrifice' reached in and touched my heart and mind.
"You're welcome and have a great day" I replied.

I turned and headed off into the park. I walked for about twenty minutes and then started to head back to the Ala Wai canal and home. I would find something to eat at my apartment, I was sure I had some peanut butter and bread in the fridge.
My walk back home took me right past that McDonald's restaurant where I had envisioned having my hash browns, egg McMuffin and coffee.
As I passed by I looked up at the picture on the large overhead sign and noticed the crisp golden hash brown

patty and a steaming cup of coffee. Torture, oh what sweet torture I thought as I walked under the sign.

I glanced over to my right at the long row of tables and chairs sitting out on the McDonald's patio shaded by a huge overhang. I started to turn away when my eye caught sight of the giant. The overalls and muscle shirt were sitting at a table with an Egg McMuffin, a beautiful golden brown hash brown patty and a steaming cup of coffee. Egad, what trick has fate played on me this day, I thought to myself, as my tummy started to rebel once again with an almost audible rebellious sound.

The growling in my stomach was starting to get threatening and I stopped and just stared. The giant did not look up he just bit down on that egg McMuffin and I could almost taste the flavor. I wonder, I thought to myself, what would happen if I walked over there and asked him if he had any spare change for a hot cup of coffee. "Nah...discard that thought" I said half out loud, "let him have his breakfast in peace" and I felt kind of neat....sort of like I did something good today and I headed home to my peanut butter sandwich and a glass of water...but my heart was singing a song of love to my Lord and my God.

"What about the 'Harvest' you ask?" (Remember the sub-title of this little story....Obedience and the Harvest....)

Parting with those five dollars was the going forward with more seed planting and the planting before the harvest....sort of like the seeds a farmer plants at the beginning of the season. He plants, the Lord provides the sunshine and the rain and God gives growth in due time. Sometimes the harvest takes quite a while to come in but with prayer and patience it will come in eventually. Having planted many a seed since I became a Christian I just watch while the rain falls, the sun shines and I know that all is working toward a decent harvest. The immediate harvest is the joy and happiness that fills my heart.

Never wanting to forget that there are years of drought, some years there is very little harvest and then there are the locusts and wind storms that affect the harvest. At times there are storms that affect our daily way of life. This is very similar to real life living. We keep faith and we pray knowing full well that eventually there will be a harvest. Storms, locusts and trials do not last forever.

That is God's promise. Let me encourage you to keep planting those seeds no matter what you feel or think....this is a faith walk, not unlike the farmer who never gives up he just keeps planning and planting year after year, through the lean years, the dry years and the years of disastrous drought....he keeps faith and he keeps planting. Well I did the same thing, I knew that one day when I needed it most my harvest would be there just as the Lord promised. Never dwelling on the harvest but just going about the business of doing what I was supposed to be doing.

Then one year, many long years after the five dollars and the Egg McMuffin incident, after I had planted another seed of faith by helping another human with love and encouragement and a few bucks, I met with disaster, a disaster that I never knew would or could materialize in my life.

I met a girl. I thought I was in love as that girl literally swept me off my feet. I was lonely, I was hungry for female companionship and I was ready to be led by the nose willingly to the altar. We married and in a short while she was cheating on me and smoking up marijuana with a guy half her age. I suppose I should have checked in with God before getting married but a lonely and hungry heart is an easy thing to twist. We stayed married for about seven months and the divorce was paralyzing to my senses. Where had I gone wrong? I thought this was a forever thing. I was devastated.

A year after the divorce, when I was sixty two years of age I was out at the ranch of a friend of mine. We saddled up two of our favorite and very spirited horses and headed out across the hills for a morning ride. I have always loved horses and could ride pretty well with the best of them. I have always been an active outdoors person. I still enjoy white water rafting even at the now age of seventy three. Anyhow back to the story. I was challenged to a race. Without hesitation I put the heels to my very willing horse's flank, bent low over his head and flew like the devil himself was after me. My horse stepped in a gopher hole and head over heels I went. I was out cold for some time and when I came to I made my way to the ranch house with the help of my buddy. An ambulance was called. I had broken my collar bone and fractured all the ribs on my right side.

The trip to the hospital took almost an hour because the ranch was quite far out in the country. Pain during

The ride? You can bet your life there was pain. The EMT was not aware that I had broken my collar bone and did not take the necessary precautions. Nonetheless I survived once again and after three days in the hospital I asked for some pain killers as I wanted to head home. I took one Extra Strength Tylenol three tablet and with a figure eight collar bone brace on my neck and shoulders I started back home. It was five hour drive but with the occasional rest time the trip took me over nine hours. I was back at work on the seventh day.

Six months after the horse riding incident I was feeling pretty bad with pains in my chest. I saw my doctor and he started treating me for indigestion. When, sometime later, I explained to him that I could not walk more than fifty feet without resting he set up a stress test for me at the local hospital. I failed the test miserably and wound up with three stents in my arteries. A month or two later I was at work and in a quiet moment I started to have pains in my chest. I waited quite a while and then when I was certain I was having a heart attack I walked into my boss's office sat in a chair and asked him to call an ambulance. His face turned white as he dialed the phone. I was three weeks in the hospital and after another angiogram I received two more stents in my arteries.

I lost my job, was divorced and I was broke. Now here I was with a broken Collar bone, fractured ribs, no job, and then I filed for bankruptcy. Filing for bankruptcy was one of the most embarrassing situations I had ever found myself in.

The whole process was demeaning. Having lost the

condominium I had purchased three years earlier, I made application and was accepted into government subsidized housing. Four hundred and fifty square feet of living space. The apartment consisted of a small but adequate bedroom. A living room/ kitchen combination and a bathroom with tub and shower.

Now where is God? I was angry and I was bitter. God, I shouted in silence, enough is enough. I am sick and tired of the way my life has turned out. Are you still there or have you forsaken me and given up on me? I asked this question so many times that I got tired of hearing my own voice. How much more God until you are done with me, how much longer until I have learned all that you want to teach me?

So do you, dear reader, think God gave up on me? I hope not because now you are going to hear the rest of the story and if you are not amazed at what happens next then I will be amazed that you are not amazed.

"Silence." That is the word that crept creeping into my mind and into my heart. Why all this silence from God? Surely there must be a reason! I am driven to try to understand God in a more meaningful way and this drives me deeper into the word of God and the name Lazarus pops into my thoughts. I open up my bible and check the concordance, my eyes fall on John Chapter 11 and I begin to read.

".....Lord the one you love is sick." With these words the sisters Mary and Martha informed Jesus that their brother Lazarus was sick. Jesus replied "This sickness will not end in death. No, it is for God's glory so that God's Son may be glorified through it." Then Jesus, instead of hurrying off to heal the 'one he loved' stayed where He was for two more days. Jesus then turned to His disciples and said "Let us go back to Judea." Then Jesus went on to say "Lazarus is dead, and for your sake I am glad I was not there, so that you may believe. But let us go to him."

Ok, now I am starting to get it in little pieces. The silence of those two days must have been very difficult for Mary and Martha, the sisters' of Lazarus. Where was Jesus, how come he did not come right away and heal their brother? Why is Jesus silent in the midst of their pain and the sickness of their brother, Lazarus? Jesus waited two days for a specific purpose...but I ask myself what is that specific purpose? Is this love? And the answer that comes to my mind is 'yes, be patient.'

God has a plan and sometimes in God's plan is the word "Silence." Between the old and new testaments there is silence for four hundred years. Was this silence because God had a plan? When I checked my bible references I find that there is absolutely no word from God for those four hundred years. Why, I ask myself and how does God's silence apply to me and my situation right now.

I turn on the television one Sunday morning and there is Pastor Charles Stanley and his usual Sunday sermon. He is speaking about the silence of God. I sit bolt upright in my chair, my eyes and ears are glued to the television set. Why this is exactly what I have been praying about these past few days.

I turn up the volume and I listen to Dr. Charles Stanley and I hear him pronounce "During God's silence we can learn some of our greatest lessons." Dr. Stanley goes on; "God's silent time is sometimes God's preparation time, He (God) is preparing something big for you.

And so as I contemplate Dr. Stanley's words, I find that sometimes I am just not ready to listen to what God has to say. Sometimes I am so busy that I miss the message that God may have sent my way ....Dr. Stanley continues; "Kneeling before God is the thing to be doing, don't let pride stand in your way and don't stop praying because God may be silent for some specific reason."

As I listen I find, through Dr. Stanley, that I have a heart problem. Now, in actuality, I do physically have a heart problem. I have five stents in my arteries, I have had a heart attack and all at once God's message to me through my television set and Dr. Stanley on that Sunday morning becomes clear. I don't need any spiritual stents in my arteries to keep my heart healthy.

I need a whole new heart because of my complaining about being in a four hundred and fifty square foot apartment with the rent subsidized by the government. I have been complaining for months and yelling at God, "Where are you?"

So I sought a heart transplant from the original 'heart giver' which is God. My problem is a weak heart. Has God not strengthened my heart over these past long years of serving Him; did God not give me the courage and strength to carry His banner during all those years, through the good times, the bad times, the drought and through the rain and storms of life? Of course He did and I have let my heart become weak and it needs to be strengthened once again. God has not forsaken me, He has been silent in order that I might also be silent and learn the lessons that He has for me.

Romans Chapter 8 verse 28 pops into my mind and I grab my bible, the word of God that never lies and I start to read. "And we know that in all things God works for the good of those who love Him.......etc." and further on I read "..........Who shall separate us from the love of Christ? Shall trouble or hardship or persecution or danger or sword? And further "........for I am convinced that neither death nor life, neither angels nor demons, neither the present nor the future, nor any powers, etc. ....will be able to separate us from the love of God that is in Christ Jesus our Lord." I read on and now the silence is deafening. God is speaking to me right this minute, right here in the midst of my misery.

Here I am broke; living in subsidized housing and during my complaining my God is teaching me a valuable lesson. In silence there is a lesson to be learned. Maybe God will be silent towards me for four hundred years or maybe a day or two or possibly eight more years. I don't care I want to learn what God wants to teach me and I will endure the silence. I get up off my knees. It is Wednesday morning and it is early. I walk into my kitchen/living room combination and I stand behind an old kitchen chair. I put my hands on back of the chair, I take a deep breath and I know I am about to lose my pride, I am about to get humble before my God and for me this is so difficult.

I start to talk to God and I tell Him that I am sorry for complaining, I tell God that from this moment on I will do my best to complain no more. I look around me and I see what God has given me. I have a bed to sleep in, I have a fridge with food in it, I have a living room and a couch to sit on and most of all I have a roof over my head. Now I am looking at God's blessings and a tear rolls down my cheek. But I am smiling and I am happy and it is Wednesday morning.

Three days after the incident that took place in my kitchen it is Saturday morning and I am suddenly One Hundred and Fifty Thousand Dollars richer....No my friend, it isn't a misprint, you read it correctly. Now I invite you to read on. I am $150,000.00 richer and I mean real money. I cannot believe my eyes. I turn the envelope over and yes, it has my name on it and it has my correct address on it. With trembling hands, I hold the cheque up before my eyes and study all the details. My name is on the cheque, my name is spelled correctly. I check the date and yes, the date is current. Weak in the knees and trembling I hold the cheque against my heart as if to show it to God. Now what would God have me do with this money, I ponder as I rejoice in this incredible miracle, a miracle that only God could work.

Putting the money into my account at the bank I find my balance is now $150,121.09. The bank personnel were amazed when I showed up with the cheque. Being a bank in a relatively small city everyone knows everyone else. There were pats on the back, comments of joy and what an opportunity for me to proclaim the goodness of God and to proclaim His name as the name that blesses all who trust in Him.

Now it is time to share with those that have needs. It was not difficult as I volunteer at a club for alcoholics and recovering alcoholics. Having once been an alcoholic myself and now sober for 33 years I am somewhat able to relate to the problems that others have with alcohol...this is my "Giving Back" as thanks for my own sobriety.

First on my list was to allow God to inspire me, in my spirit, who I could share this money with. My brother Patrick, who lives in California, comes first and foremost to my mind. I got hold of his bank account number and deposited directly into his account Ten Thousand Dollars. When Patrick was next in his bank on business and checked the balance of his account he was, to his surprise, $10,000.00 richer. But wait, hold on a minute, wait until you hear the rest of this story and the $10,000.00

My brother is a Viet Nam veteran. Patrick and I were in the Canadian navy together and when we were discharged he went and crossed the border into the USA and joined the Marine Corps. He was almost two years in Vietnam and came home a well decorated hero. As an aside, although Patrick is exactly one year younger than me I have always thought of his as my hero and a very, very courageous hero at that. I have nothing but admiration and love for my brother.

That doesn't mean that while growing up we didn't have our difference that sometimes led into a physical brawl or two. Let me share a childhood incident with you. Patrick and I were playing darts one afternoon. Darts were a common activity at our home. It seems that all of the family and extended family loved to play darts. Well anyhow Patrick and I were shooting darts and it was my turn to try and hit the bull's eye. I shot the three darts and I think I came close to the bull's eye.

One of the darts that I threw hit the wire rim of the dart board and bounced onto the floor in front of the dart board. I walked over to retrieve my darts and when I bent down to pick up the one on the floor the temptation for Patrick to hit a human bull's eye was too much for him to resist. Patrick threw the dart and true to its mark it flew....right into my chubby little rear end. The dart hurt like heck and pulling it out hurt even more. Then the fight started.

Ok, back to the bank and the $10,000.00. Patrick called me a few days later and related the following story to me which I hold to be the absolute truth. Terry, he says, you will never guess what happened. And he told me this story.

My brother lives in a Mobile home in Southern California. He has a pension from the Military but does not have a lot of money. It seems the fellow that Patrick purchased the mobile home from dropped by to pick up the mortgage payment. Patrick asked him what the balance was on the mortgage. The owner said, after checking his figures, you owe a balance of $8,989.00. Well Patrick almost fell out of his chair when he heard the figure.

You see when I mailed that money order, in Canadian funds, to his bank and they took the exchange the difference between the Canadian Funds and the American funds was exactly $8989.00. Terry, says Patrick over the telephone, I paid off my mortgage right to the penny. Well we both spent considerable time on the telephone rejoicing in just what God can do. Patrick's final statement to me before we hung up the telephone was; Terry, God has blessed you and through you he is blessing others." I liked that thought.

I have numerous short, but happy stories to tell and I will save them for another time. Possibly one day we might meet and I will be able to share some of them with you. I think they will make your heart happy and point you in a more positive way to the goodness and graciousness of God and His Son, Jesus.

I sent my ex wife, whom I had not seen for thirty years, $5,000 dollars and my son $3,000 dollars. I assisted my other son, Mike, to the tune of about $4,000 dollars and then I sought ways to spend God's money that would please God. I bought a neat little used mobile home (1,100 sq. ft. with two bedrooms and two bathrooms) and then I furnished it. I bought a new car and gave my old one to a friend who needed transportation. I spent two weeks in Hawaii and took a seven day Alaskan cruise. All in all I attempted to spend the money in any way that I thought would please God. (With a few perks for myself) I figured if God gave me the money then He wanted me to share it or as my brother, Paddy, stated above "Terry, God has blessed you and through you he is blessing others." I still like that thought.

Ok, ok you talked me into it. Here is one other short story that is both happy and sad. When I was volunteering at the club for alcoholics, an aged man came into the club one day. He was obviously underweight and looked pretty pathetic in his manner of dress. His clothes were tattered and soiled. His shoes had seen better days. The leather on one of them was starting to peel off and he had on two different colored socks. One sock was bright red and was a thick winter sock. The other was stripped blue and black and was a summer type sock. On his face was about three day's growth of beard.

"Come on in" I greeted him as he stepped through the door. "How are you," I asked as he took a seat. When he sat it was obvious that he was a weary traveler. "Oh I'm doing fine." He stated. I am tired from travelling and I sure could use a cup of coffee." I got him his coffee and offered him a piece of cake that was left over from one of the meetings. He took the cake, and as he drank his coffee I could see the life coming back into his eyes. He told me his name was Jake. Well Jake and I talked for about an hour and I learned that he had just hit town after a Greyhound bus ride from a city about a thousand miles away.

He told me that he had a brother in town that was going to give him a job and he looked forward to starting over. After a phone call and about two hours of waiting his brother picked him up and off they went. A few days later Jake came in and was pretty well cleaned up. He had on clean blue jeans, a used, but excellent pair of shoes and he was clean shaven.

"Thanks for your kindness, I appreciate it" were the first words out of his mouth and I could see a weak smile forming on his face. "That's great" I exclaimed, "but you don't seem very happy."
"Oh, I'm happy, except for one thing."

"What's that?" I asked.

He frowned, hesitated and said, "I don't have my driver's license."

"How come?" I enquired.

"Well I haven't had it for seven years due to the fact that I owe the license people $785 dollars and until I pay that I won't have it."

I turned to one of the other guys that was sitting playing cribbage and asked him to watch the club for an hour. "Where are you going," he asked? As Jake had gone to the washroom I confided that I was going to help Jake get his license. Robert, that was the name of the fellow that I asked to watch the club, stood up, took me aside and told me that Jake had only a few months to live as he had advanced cancer. I asked how he knew that and he said that Jake's brother was a friend of his and had confided that information to him.

He also stated that Jake wanted his driver's license more than anything in this world. For Jake his license was his identification as a citizen. His driver's license gave him authenticity and acceptability into society. Robert went on to say that Jake had been praying for months and months to just have his driver's license. I thanked Robert and told him to keep an eye on the club as Jake and I would be back in an hour.

I returned to the club and let the guys know that Jake was one happy guy. His fines were paid and he would have his license in a few days. They asked me what Jake said about the whole thing. I swallowed hard, took a deep breath and told them what Jake said....he said nothing…he just stood there with the receipt in his hand and he cried.

Three days later Jake showed up at the club grinning from ear to ear. Flashing his newly acquired license with his photo on it he showed it to everyone in the club. There were the usual jokes about the photo and congratulations were offered to Jake.

He thanked all the guys, gave me a hug and walked out the door with that grin on his face and holding his license up in front of him.

Justin, Jake's brother dropped in two weeks later and let us know that Jake wasn't feeling well and they had taken him to the hospital. Robert said that when they put Jake into a bed Jake held something in his hand and no prompting from the nurses or doctor would make him let go of it. It was his driver's license. Robert also told us that Jake slept with the license under his pillow and when he woke the next day he ate breakfast, sitting up in bed with his driver's license in his hand. Three days later Jake died and his only request was that he be allowed to be buried with his driver's license. The family all agreed and Jake was laid to rest clutching his license in his hand.

Justin said that he thought he had detected a faint smile on Jake's face just as they were closing the casket. Terry, Justin addressed me, you will never really know the depth of happiness that you gave Jake the day you paid his fines and allowed him to get his license. That driver's license meant everything to Jake. Well, my dear reader God did the whole thing and as my brother said, "Terry God blessed you and through you He is blessing others." I still like that thought. Sure there were those at the club that thought I was crazy for spending $785 on a dying man...but what do I care what they thought. My feeling is this...."Does God think I'm crazy?" Sure hope not.

Plant a seed reap a harvest. Plant a seed of happiness and reap a harvest of joy. It's not really all about money. God has many fields just waiting for a seed to be sown. Seeds of friendship and get a harvest of friends. Plant a seed of a smile and reap a bountiful harvest of smiles. I could go on and on but I'll let you fill in the other seeds that could be sown, by you personally, and let you think about the harvest in your life. Remember what I said earlier...God's promise is exactly like gravity...it never fails.

You can work out the details any way that pleases you. You can, like me, thank God or you can find fault in all this. The choice is yours. As for me, in my silence, I learned a valuable lesson and that was to stop complaining and be grateful for all things. Thank you God for never leaving me nor forsaking me, just as you promised.

Now let's spend a few more minutes on your harvest. Ok, so you don't hang out at the park in Waikiki so the chances of you spotting a huge rear end hanging out of a dumpster is pretty slim, but wait a minute farming and bringing in a harvest takes many forms. How about surrogate farming, you know where you put up the money and someone else does the farming.

Today we call that tithing. That is where you sit in

church or you see a group or organization feeding the poor, helping the homeless, administering medication and first aid to people who have been through or are going through a disaster. And that disaster doesn't have to be in some foreign country it could be right around the corner.

So there you are sitting in church and the pastor is talking about building an extension to the church to help school the youngsters and others about a better life style that includes God. You know the God that you also worship because that is why you are in church.

And as you listen the Pastor is talking about that little hardly known group of church folks that are going downtown to feed the homeless. Ooooops is this a place to be a surrogate farmer, is this the place to plant that seed to bring in your harvest?

Someone, an elder in the church, steps up to the podium and standing beside him is a rather bedraggled looking man. His pants are a little too big, his shirt is ill fitting and his shoes are obviously not new. But he stands there with the biggest and most beautiful smile on his face and somehow you notice that there is a glow about him. He starts to talk and his voice and countenance show an enormous understanding of love for those less fortunate. He tells about being in prison for sixteen years...he tells the congregation about the horrors of prison and how, one day, he hung himself in the darkened corner of his filthy cell. He woke up in the prison hospital with bandages around his neck and he was shackled to the hospital bed. A guard by accident, by chance, or by a loving gesture sent as an angel from God had passed his cell at that precise moment and seeing this useless body hanging in a corner....he cut it down...and the body breathed life once again.

Then the speaker talks about telling the doctor that he wanted to die and would he, the doctor, please give him an injection so could die. The doctor, a Christian man, gave him an injection all right but it was a verbal tongue lashing injection that sent his mind reeling. The convict slept and when he awoke the next morning, there stood the smiling face of the prison Chaplain.

They talked and talked and the prisoner asked plenty of questions. The answers he got were simple, not complicated and they spoke of a loving God who gave His son to pay the penalty for the sins of all mankind and in a moment that hardened criminal, who a few days before was hanging from a filthy tied knot in a prison cell, went from criminal to freedom. His mind was clear because he understood what it meant to have someone pay your fine so you could go free. Once the fine was paid, the penalty satisfied then freedom followed. Well that once hardened criminal, now standing at that church podium talks about accepting Jesus as his Savior, a fine paid and freedom follows. He speaks of Jesus, on the cross, between two thieves. One thief acknowledges Jesus as the Savior of the world and Jesus says to him, "This day you will be with me in heaven." Jesus paid the final payment for this man's freedom for all eternity.

Next this ex convict he tells about the chaplain who came to visit him and how, when his time was served, this prison chaplain brought him clothes to wear. A clean shirt that the chaplain's wife had washed and ironed, clean pants, underwear, socks and a raincoat.

The day he walked out of prison this prison chaplain met him and got him into a half way house. He has never looked back. Today, he explains, he is employed and giving back to the community that he harmed so many years ago and, as he states, he walks with his hand in the hand of God all day, every day.

Giving, my friend, is one of the best farming practices I can think of for those with a loving willing heart but just can't seem to find the time to check out the dumpsters in Hawaii. Your schedule is busy, you have meetings, money to earn to support your family, errands to run, children to raise. Your family is precious to you and they come first and well they should. But don't give up farming or giving God a chance to help you bring in that harvest.

Wiggle yourself around a little the next time you are in church and dig out that wallet. Don't be afraid to let go of that five or ten dollar bill because it represents a seed that you are planting. And when you plant that seed do it with a smile and watch the immediate harvest of smiles that you bring in.

The Chaplain and all those others will take that few bucks and add it to the dollars and cents that others are giving and it becomes one great big seed planting party as they feed the homeless, bind up the wounded and provide a loving secure place for thousands of folks that need our help. Don't do it just for the harvest but do it because it is the loving Christian thing to do...if don't believe me about all this...well take a minute out, read your bible and have a chat with God. You might find that still clear voice is just waiting to talk with you. If your seed planting brings in a bountiful harvest for some senior citizen that needs a sandwich or a youngster who just needs some love then you have reaped a harvest that will produce more seeds and then those seeds will produce another harvest.

By the way you just might be surprised some morning when you wake up to find that a harvest has come up in your own back yard. And oh yes....Those seeds that I planted most of my life...and that harvest, well ....I kind of think it came up in my own back yard, in God's perfect time. Thank you Jesus.

Where is a good place to start, you might ask? Let me tell you where I started. I didn't start giving because I was sitting in a church. ....no that was not necessary....I started giving because it just felt like the right thing to do. What about the harvest? Well let me explain something to you that you may not have thought of before.

That harvest I talk about is exactly the same as gravity....it is a law. It is God's law and God's promise that He will bless, in abundance, those who give generously. Now giving generously does not mean to imply that you have to give all your money away, no not at all. The bible speaks of how happy and pleased God was with a widow who gave just a wee bit of money out of her meager income. Maybe it was dime or a nickel. God doesn't necessarily need your money in order to bless you in abundance; He wants the abundance of love from your heart.

Even a convict in prison can give if he wants to. Just take a dollar and mail it to some group that is ministering

God's love and blessing to others. Or how about smile of encouragement to someone who just landed in prison for the first time. My friend that is sowing seeds and I can guarantee you a bountiful harvest.

A street person can plant a seed...instead of bumming a few bucks off someone and turning that money into cigarettes, dope or booze...why not take a little and pass it on...say you get five dollars on the street...how about just dropping into some church or Christian organization and passing on one of those dollars, or fifty cents or a quarter. But hear this loud and clear....Do it with love. Don't give with one hand while you are holding the other hand out for something in return. Just plant that seed with a loving heart and let God deal with the harvest His way and in His time. That is planting a seed...you will get the promise of God and the harvest as sure as you will experience the law of gravity every time you take a step.

Sure, your harvest may not come in the next day, but it will come in. I planted my five dollar seed at the dumpster in Hawaii and other places and I never expected one cent in return. I was happy to help wherever and whenever I could...it just plain feels good. But my seed planting did bring in a harvest but it took something like thirty or forty years and as sure as gravity has never failed me neither has God. My harvest came in exactly on time and at the perfect moment that is God's timing at work. He is ever faithful; you can bet your boots on it. You think Wall Street investing is generous...check out God's Wall Street...it is called tithing or giving and it can, as God sees fit bring enormous returns. Don't do it for the money, do it for the love of God's creation... leave the results to God.

It is my sincere prayer that one day you too will open an envelope just as I did when God blessed me and find yourself staring at a cheque for $150,000.00. I cannot even write how I felt at that moment because I do not know the proper words to express those feelings. Sure I gave almost all of it away...but that is what started the whole thing in the first place. And I found that Obedience and a Harvest go hand in hand. Kind of like gravity...it is God's law and it never fails.

The reason I have not mentioned how God blessed me with $150,000.00 is because I want you to concentrate on what God wants you to do, as an individual, and not follow what I did. Maybe one day, if we meet, I will tell you the rest of the story.

A little about the bankruptcy that I had filed. After I had that money in my bank account and the bankruptcy was way behind me I knew that I still had an obligation to do the right thing. I called the people who held the mortgage on my condominium when I filed bankruptcy and asked them what they had lost on the re-sale of my home. The figure they quoted me was just over $5,000.00. I sat down and sent them a cheque for that exact amount. Someone told me that I did not have to do that as the bankruptcy had covered any loss. Possibly so, but one thing I knew for sure I was just giving them back their money.

Next I called the company that I had a leased pickup truck from and asked them what my filing bankruptcy had cost them. When they gave me the figure I sat down and wrote out a cheque for that amount and put it in the mail. They were so surprised and grateful that they even discounted what they lost and gave me a break of a few hundred dollars....also mentioning, as the people that lost money on my condominium did.... that they had never heard of anyone going back after filing bankruptcy and paying the losses. Well they just never ran into me before. And so I did with the others that got hurt financially when I filed my bankruptcy...I called each one and paid off the debt. Now I am not saying this is what everyone should do under similar circumstances...I am only saying that is what I did. By the way, it was a real good feeling.

So, my friends, there you have my story and I hope somehow I have inspired you to start giving away some smiles, friendship, and a sandwich occasionally to a hungry person. Don't forget a firm handshake and a compliment occasionally....Plant the seeds and as sure as gravity never fails neither will the promises of God.

Oh yes, one last thought. Always be aware of this...if you are married make sure that you both agree on which seeds to plant, which field to plant them in, particularly if you are sowing a financial seed.

Why, you might ask? Simple answer....."And the two shall become one." (Check out Ephesians Chapter five verse 31....Ephesians 5:31). Why is this important well my friend if there is no harmony in choosing when, where, how, and in what field to plant the seeds how in heavens name can God decide to allow a bountiful harvest. Should God bless the wife, say 72% and then bless the husband 28% or vice versa? In essence they are not "One" any more, at least not on this issue....they are 'Split'...or agreeably they are "Two."

Have you ever heard of a farmer who is sowing seeds to bring in a bountiful harvest, planting one seed in one place and another seed in a different place? Of course not. Did you really think God did not know what He was talking about when He said a husband and wife shall become one? Wife to be obedient to her husband and a husband willing to lay down his life for his wife. Ok, maybe the wife doesn't like the word obedience... well maybe the husband doesn't like the word death but he, the husband, must accept the fact that he is called to protect his wife even unto death.

Now if I have stepped too far out of bounds then take it up with God...He said it, and like gravity, the harvest and God's word and promises never fail. If the husband and wife can't agree on when, where or how to plant a financial seed then the best thing to do is do nothing. Wait until God settles the right time, place and manner to sow a financial seed that you both can agree on and honor God. Waiting never hurt anyone but over zealousness has ruined many a friendship and marriage, particularly if it is over money.

"Ok, Terrence so what's with all this God stuff?" Well some folks think that a space ship dropped us off here on earth (not so far fetched) that someone would think this way, for I heard these words directly from the mouth of a friend). Others believe that somehow we humans slipped out of a pile of slime and ooze somewhere in a swamp (ever wonder where the swamp came from?) Others are convinced that we are descendants of monkeys or gorillas.....has anyone ever dug up a half monkey/half human. Sorry friend, the evidence is sorely lacking. That is probably why Evolution is just a THEORY...and devoid of irrefutable fact. Remember that your theory and my theory are absolute as long as we don't have to produce absolute evidence that CANNOT be refuted.

The evidence for CREATION and that there is a GOD is perfectly irrefutable. No, I'm not going to argue this point with you or anyone else. What is your task? The research and evidence gathering to either prove or disprove that God does exist and that you and I are or are not created beings. I like the thought of being created and not being something that oozed out of a slimy pit.

So, my friend having that belief snugly tucked under my belt (so to speak) and deeply imbedded in my heart and spirit, let me now give you something to ponder from a Creator who loves you and me. Just read on for a few more minutes....you won't be sorry you did and it just might change your life....forever. Here are some of the promises of the one who loves you and if you want rest of the story....go read a bible....

**"But remember this - if you give a little, you will get a little. A farmer who plants just a few seeds will get only a small crop, but if he plants much, he will reap much. Everyone must make up his own mind as to how much he should give. Don't force anyone to give more than he really wants to, for cheerful givers are the ones God prizes.

God is able to make it up to you by giving you everything that you need and more. So that there will not only be enough for your own needs, but plenty left over to give joyfully to others. The Godly man gives generously to the poor. His good deeds will be an honor to him forever. For God who gives seed to the farmer to plant, and later on, good crops to harvest and eat, will give you more and more fruit from your harvest. Yes, God will give you much so you can give away much. And when your gifts are given to them that need them they will break out into thanksgiving and praise to God for your love and help. So two good things happen as a result of your gifts [seed planting of money, food, smiles, encouragement love and much more] - Those in need are helped, and they overflow with thanks to God."** The Living Bible 2nd Corinthians 9:6-12

Ok, go on out there and start planting and while you are sowing those seeds keep a smile on your face and enjoy yourself.

God Bless you, and Happy Farming
Terrence Morrissey

CPSIA information can be obtained at www.ICGtesting.com
Printed in the USA
LVOW06s0331060614

388804LV00001B/3/P

9 781467 044127